Tales from
Near and Far

Jacqueline Dembar Greene
Illustrated by Martin Melango
and Diana Kizlauskas

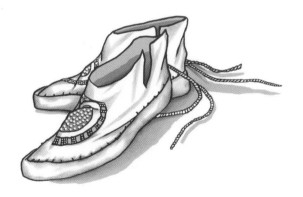

A Harcourt Achieve Imprint

www.Rigby.com
1-800-531-5015

Literacy by Design Leveled Readers: *Tales from Near and Far*

Illustration credits:
Martin Melango p. 26-27, 28, 29, 30, 31, 32-33, 34, 36, 37, 38-39,
40-41, 42, 44, 46, 47, 48;
Diana Kizlauskas cvr, p. 1, 3, 4, 6-7, 8, 9, 10, 12-13, 15, 16-17, 19,
20-21, 22, 23, 24

ISBN-13: 978-1-4189-3794-2
ISBN-10: 1-4189-3794-0

Printed in China
1B 2 3 4 5 6 7 8 985 13 12 11 10 09 08 07

Contents

Spider Grandmother and the Footrace:
A Hopi Tale

1
Running Deer

Long ago, two villages stood side by side. Tikuvi was a large village with rich cornfields and many men to work them. Payupki was tiny, but the people there were happy and lived a peaceful life.

One day the Payupki chief passed Tikuvi and saw men running. He saw that Tikuvi had swift runners and knew they would become faster as they trained. He returned to his own village and sent for Running Deer, a young boy who was the village's fastest messenger. The boy could run for hours without tiring.

"Running Deer," the chief said, "Tikuvi men are training. They will challenge us to a footrace when they feel they're ready. You are our fastest runner. Go to Tikuvi and practice with them. Watch carefully, work hard, but do not show how fast you are."

When Running Deer arrived in Tikuvi, he was welcomed. He ran in the longest footrace so he could see how strong the runners were. The footracers started with a burst of speed. Running Deer was far behind, but he kept his pace steady and tried to watch while he ran.

The men from Tikuvi began to tire. As they fell back, Running Deer moved ahead. Soon there were just two runners in front of him. He passed the second one. When he was close on the heels of the lead runner, he knew he could overtake him. But Running Deer remembered his task. He was not in Tikuvi to show his skills. He slowed down and allowed the man to win the race. When he returned home, Running Deer talked with the chief. "I came in second," he said, "but I think I could have won if I had run my fastest."

"That's what I needed to know," the chief said. "Tikuvi will soon challenge us to a race. You must practice to make yourself even faster."

2

Spider Grandmother's Unwanted Advice

Every morning and evening, Running Deer trained. He ran across the flat mesa, high above the desert floor. He climbed down to the fields where the cattle grazed and ran across the hot sand of the desert. He raced up and down the slopes of the hills.

One day the Tikuvi chief called upon the Payupki chief. The two men sat in a kiva, a house where ceremonies and meetings were held.

"In four days, Tikuvi will hold a race. Come with your best runners, and we shall offer prizes to the village with the swiftest runner."

"My village is small," the Payupki chief said. "We have only the young boy you have seen. But we shall enter him in the race."

The night before the race, the Tikuvi chief called the village leaders to the kiva. They argued about whether or not to offer their possessions as prizes in the race. But the chief was not concerned.

"You have seen their best runner already," the chief reminded them. "Running Deer didn't win when he practiced with us. He will not win the race."

While they were talking, Spider Grandmother came down to the ladder into the kiva.

"Go away," the men called. "Only men meet here."

Spider Grandmother tried to ignore their insult. "I have come to help our runners win the race."

But the men were no longer worried. "We don't need your advice," they said. "Go away, Grandmother."

"When you need me, I always help. Now you tell me to leave. That is what I shall do." She gathered her possessions and left the village.

But the men of Tikuvi took no notice. They were busy preparing for the race, planning which men would run.

Spider Grandmother walked to Payupki. The villagers welcomed her and led her to their kiva. Here the leaders were also discussing their runner's chances in the race. When they saw the old woman coming down the ladder, they called to her.

"Come and join us, Grandmother. Why are you here?"

She spoke honestly. "I tried to help the men in my village find ways to win the race. But they do not want my advice. They told me to leave. So I have come to help you."

The chief thanked her. "What advice do you have for us, Grandmother?" he asked.

"The people of Tikuvi will celebrate tonight. They are sure of their victory. Tomorrow they will be tired. Make sure that your runner sleeps," Grandmother replied.

"You are wise, Grandmother," the chief told her. "We shall do what you say."

When the meeting was over, the leaders found a place for Grandmother to stay. Villagers brought her warm blankets, cooking pots, and corn. They stacked wood and started a fire for her.

The next morning, the Payupki villagers went to the racing grounds. Running Deer walked ahead of them. A young man collected the things that the villagers had brought for the prizes. Arrow points, beaded moccasins, blankets, deer-bone necklaces, and rugs lay in a pile. The winning village would get everything.

Running Deer raced well. He ran against Tikuvi runners in long-distance runs. He ran against their runners for short distances. Running Deer won every race. The Payupki men cheered, while the Tikuvi men scowled. The Payupki men tossed Running Deer into the air.

After the feast that followed, the Payupki villagers collected their prizes. They returned home, placed their winnings in front of Spider Grandmother, and allowed her to choose whatever she wished. Then they gave some of the prizes to Running Deer. The villagers shared the rest of the winnings.

3

Running Girl

Some days later, the Payupki chief called for Running Deer. "The Tikuvi men are poor losers," he said. "I know they will challenge us to another race soon. You must not let your success make you lazy. You must train even harder to be ready for the next race."

Running Deer rose before dawn each day and ran through the village, through the fields, and across the mesa.

One morning his sister said, "I have watched you, and you are slow. You must learn to run faster. Tomorrow I will run with you and help you."

The next day, Running Deer and his sister raced. She called to him as she ran by easily, "Keep your head up. Use your legs, my brother." They ran the same course each day, yet when Running Deer finished, he found his sister already at home, grinding corn.

"Aren't you tired?" he asked.

"That was nothing," his sister said. "I can run faster than that."

The Tikuvi chief again met with the Payupki chief. He invited Payupki to another race day. "We must have a chance to win back what we lost," he said. When the Tikuvi chief left, the Payupki chief met with Running Deer.

"We are again counting on you to be the fastest," the Payupki chief said. Running Deer shook his head.

"I am not the fastest runner in the village," he explained. "I have been training with my sister, and she always beats me. She must race for us."

So the villagers of Payupki sent a message to Tikuvi. "In four days, we shall race with you. But our racer will be Running Girl."

The village women were pleased. They would all go watch Running Girl challenge the men. It would be a festive day.

The Tikuvi men were nervous. "If Payupki has a faster runner than Running Deer, how will we win? Running Deer has already beaten our swiftest racers. Ask Spider Grandmother for help!" But Spider Grandmother's house was empty. They didn't know where she had gone.

Payupki's villagers gave Spider Grandmother gifts of food. They asked for her help, and she willingly gave it.

"Tikuvi people are poor losers," she said. "They will cheat to win. If needed, I will turn myself into a spider and sit on Running Girl's head. I will watch for danger and help her."

4

The Dove, the Hawk, and the Spider

When race day came, the villagers stood beside the racing grounds. Men piled up their prizes of arrow points, bows, quivers, and moccasins. Women offered pots, blankets, baskets, and strings of beads. It looked like a mountain of gifts!

Running Girl tightened her moccasins. She tucked her skirt into her belt. When the first race began, she took the lead, running past barrel cactus and pointed yucca. She ran past rock formations that jutted from the desert. And she ran past every runner from Tikuvi. The second race ended just like the first.

Before the third race, the Tikuvi villagers knew it was their last chance to win. They chose their fastest runner and decided that he alone would race against Running Girl. Everyone stood at the starting line to cheer them on. But Spider Grandmother sensed trouble. She turned herself into a spider and sat on Running Girl's head. When the race began, she urged Running Girl on. "Faster, Granddaughter! Run faster!"

Running Girl ran like the wind, and soon she couldn't see the Tikuvi runner behind her. Over her head, though, flew a dove.

"So," Spider Grandmother said, "their runner has turned into a dove. He will fly to the finish to beat you."

Spider Grandmother called to a hawk. It swooped down and chased the dove away. Running Girl sped past. When the dove returned, Spider Grandmother again called the hawk, and again it chased the dove away. Running Girl raced toward the finish.

As they neared the cheering crowd, the dove turned itself back into a man. He could not overtake Running Girl, though. The race was over, and Payupki had won again.

5

Spider Grandmother's Welcome Advice

All during the feast that followed, the Tikuvi people were quiet. They did not like losing. For them, nothing seemed worse than losing, except losing twice. They watched jealously as the Payupki people collected their winnings.

That night, as the chief offered the first gifts to Spider Grandmother and Running Girl, the old woman spoke to the village. "I know the people of Tikuvi are plotting against us," she said. "They plan to take back all their winnings. They are planning war against us."

The peaceful Payupki villagers were afraid. "We have too few men to fight," they said. "What can we do?"

"We must leave this place tomorrow," Spider Grandmother said. "I will lead you to a place where we will be safe."

That night, the people tied all of their belongings into bundles. They wrapped their cooking pots and grinding stones in blankets. Mothers tied their babies against their backs. Before the first light of day, the villagers began their journey. Behind them, nothing was left in the village, not even a feather.

Spider Grandmother led them down the mesa, along a trail they had never seen before. The Payupki traveled with their cattle across the canyon, stopping only to fill their water gourds and to let the cattle drink from the stream. For four days they walked, leaving their jealous neighbors behind.

At last, Spider Grandmother led the people to a beautiful spot near a river. They built a new village there. The best house went to Spider Grandmother, and the next best to Running Deer and Running Girl. The people named their new village Payupki in honor of the village they had left behind, and forever lived there in peace.

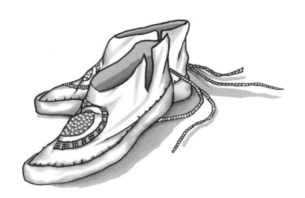

Paco Sees Three:
A Story from Old Spain

1
Paco Leaves Home

Paco lived with his mother and brothers and sisters in a village in Spain. His mother worked hard washing her neighbors' laundry to earn enough money for food.

Paco was the oldest child, but instead of helping his mother by chopping wood for the fire that boiled the wash water, he played tricks on his friends. Instead of helping to wring out the wet laundry or hang the clothes to dry, he practiced his tricks. Each day he slept late, and when he finally got up, he sat around perfecting his tricks.

"I'm so clever," he announced, "that I will travel the world and make my fortune." He promised his mother he would return some day with enough money to care for the whole family.

Paco's mother wasn't sorry to see her son leave. He was no help at all, and now she had one less mouth to feed. She wished him luck and returned to her work.

Paco traveled to a village where people didn't know what a trickster he was. He sat down in the market square and invited people to play Find the Pea. On top of an old barrel he set a dried pea under one of three walnut shells, quickly moved them into different positions, and asked for one coin if the player couldn't guess which shell hid the pea. No matter how carefully the villagers watched, Paco was too quick for their eyes. Paco fooled everyone who placed a coin on the table. His pockets were soon filled with coins, but people became angry whenever Paco set up his game.

"He is a wizard," one man whispered. Others spread the rumor. "Yes, he uses magical powers to make the pea disappear." It didn't take long before Paco found that none were willing to play. He moved to the next town to find new people to trick.

He set himself up in the square wearing an old blue robe and a silk turban he brought from home. For two coins, he promised to make the pea under the shell disappear, then reappear where he chose.

In this new town, people flocked to the square to see Paco work his magic. He never failed to please the crowd. One day, however, a man placed three coins on Paco's barrel.

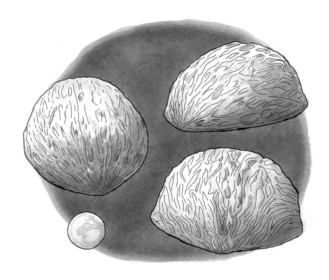

"If you're a wizard," he said, "tell me if my crop will be large this year. Should I plant wheat or tomatoes?"

Paco closed his eyes. He rubbed his forehead. He waved his hands mysteriously in front of his face. At last he spoke.

"Rain will come and crops will grow.
Tomatoes and wheat, both you must sow."

The man went away thinking he had spent his coins wisely. "Now I know the future," the man boasted.

Days stretched into weeks, and Paco pretended to look into the future for others. He often spoke in rhymes and riddles and was careful to leave before any of his predictions could prove to be false.

As spring turned to summer, Paco decided it was time to move on. He hired a tailor to sew stars and shining pieces of shell on his robe, made himself a long walking stick, and headed for the large city of Seville.

2
The Great Wizard

Along the way, Paco helped himself to sweet grapes in the vineyards. He picked tomatoes from the fields. When he reached Seville, he stopped at an inn and announced that he was Paco the Great, who could see into the past and future.

The innkeeper looked into Paco's dark eyes and decided to treat this stranger with respect. She gave him her finest room, piled his plate with the choicest pieces of meat at every meal, and spread the word that Paco the Great stayed at her inn.

It happened that on the day Paco arrived in Seville, all the king's silver plates and cups disappeared. The king was a volcano of anger—how could he be expected to eat his meals from ordinary wooden plates? He must have silver for his food!

He ordered his people to find the thieves who had taken his silver, and make certain that every piece was returned at once! The king's advisors questioned the maids, the cooks, and the guards, but no one had seen the king's silver. Then one of the advisors made a suggestion.

"Your Majesty, a wizard has come to Seville. He claims to see a person's past and future. Perhaps he can find your silver."

The king's eyes sparkled. This amazing wizard sounded like just the man he needed, and he sounded entertaining as well. He called Paco to the palace.

Paco bowed to the king, then stood nervously in his robe, his hands shaking under the wide sleeves.

"So, you are Paco the Great," the king chuckled. "You look like a boy to me. We shall see if you truly have magical powers, or if you are just a rascal."

"I shall serve Your Majesty," Paco said. He didn't feel as brave as he had in the square, and he worried that the king wouldn't be as easy to fool.

"Some thief has stolen the silver plates and cups from the castle," the king began. "None of my advisors can find the rascal. Since you see the past and the future, I command you to prove yourself by finding my silver."

Paco felt his throat tighten. "It will take time, Your Majesty." He swept his arm at everyone in the room. "I foresee that the silver will be found."

"Indeed it will," the king said, "or you will pay with your life. And to make things interesting, you shall be locked in the dungeon. That shouldn't be a problem for you, should it?" Paco's knees began to knock. But the king wasn't finished. "If you don't find my silver in three days, you shall be punished as an example to anyone else who pretends to be something he is not."

3
The King's Dungeon

Guards marched Paco down to the dungeon. They unlocked a heavy door studded with nails, and they led Paco down slippery stone steps, deep into the darkness.

An old guard rattled a large ring of keys and shoved Paco into a dirty cell. There was only a wooden bench for a bed. The jailer slammed the door of the cell behind him and turned the key in the lock. High, high above him, Paco saw a bit of sunlight trickling through a small barred window. He blinked his eyes in the dim cell.

"I brought this upon myself with my trickery," he thought. "If only I can find a way out, I shall return to my mother and work hard to help her. I have wasted my entire life."

Daylight faded, but Paco could not think of a way out of his problem. How could he find the king's silver while he was locked in the dungeon? He felt weak with hunger, for he hadn't eaten all day. Just then, the guard unlocked the door and brought in a tray of food. There was a bowl of thin porridge, a crust of stale bread, and a mug of water.

"At the inn, I was given the best food the cook could prepare," Paco said.

"Just be glad you have any food at all," the guard answered. He set the tray on the bench and left.

Paco sighed. A full day had passed, and he had only two days left. He glanced at the darkening window and said softly,

"The day is gone, as is the sun.
Of all three, there goes one."

The guard looked alarmed and nearly ran from the cell. Up the stairs he bounded, as if someone were chasing him. He huddled in a storage room with two other guards.

"It's true the wizard can see a man's past," he whispered. "When I brought his food, he knew that I was one of three thieves who had taken the silver! We must confess and beg Paco to save us from the king."

But the others didn't believe him. "You imagine things," one said.

"No one can see a person's past," said the other. "I will deliver his food tomorrow. Then we'll know."

By the end of the second day, Paco had nearly given up hope. As hard as he tried, he couldn't think of a plan to save himself. He hoped the king would change his mind and tell Paco it had all been a joke.

But when the guard brought his poor supper, Paco saw the light fading from the window. Two whole days had passed. He sighed,

"The sun has set, and so it's true.
Of the three, I've now seen two."

The guard ran from the cell and raced up the stairs to find his companions. They hid in the empty storage room.

"We are discovered!" the second guard cried. Sweat poured from his forehead. "The great wizard knows that I am also a thief! We must confess and beg him to save us!"

But the third thief was not convinced. "You are both crazy," he scoffed. "You are so filled with guilt that you imagine you are caught. No man can see another man's past. Tomorrow I shall take the wizard his food, and I will prove it."

Poor Paco knew nothing of such talk. He sat alone in his cell on the third day.

"If only I had helped my family," he thought sadly. "If only I had tried to make an honest living, I wouldn't be here now." He tried to think of some way he might save himself, but all his ideas seemed to have flown out the window like so many buzzing flies.

That evening Paco didn't feel hungry. He was so worried about what might happen the next morning, he knew he couldn't swallow a crumb, even if they sent a plate of the finest food.

When the guard came, he stared at Paco, and Paco thought the man felt sorry for him. He gave a sigh and said,

"If only my mother were here with me,
I'd tell her that now I've seen all three."

The guard almost fainted at Paco's words. He ran to his thieving friends.

"We're caught!" he cried. "We must beg forgiveness, or tomorrow we will die in Paco's place."

Each man took choice food from the kitchen and pretended it was for the wizard's last meal. But in Paco's cell, they fell to the floor and begged him not to tell the king of their guilt.

"Spare us," said the first, "and we'll serve you for the rest of your days."

"Spare us," said the second, "and we'll never question your wisdom."

"Spare us," said the third, "and we'll speak of your greatness to everyone we meet."

Paco cleverly pretended he had expected this to happen. He looked down upon the thieves at his feet.

"First, bring the stolen silver to this cell. Let no one see you." The thieves nodded their heads near the cold dirt floor.

"Next, you must never steal again. If you do, I'll know, and you'll be punished. Finally, you must obey me for the rest of your days."

"Yes!" they promised.

4

Paco Returns

The next morning, the king summoned Paco. The guards marched him up from the dungeon, through the empty corridors, and into the Great Hall.

The king smiled. "Have you found my silver?"

Paco bowed. "The silver is in my cell," he said, "but the thieves are gone and won't be found."

The king sent men down to the dungeon, and they returned with silver plates and cups. They placed them at the king's feet.

"You *are* a great wizard," said the king. "Anything you wish shall be granted."

Paco said, "I only have one wish, Your Majesty. I wish to return to my own village and to my family." Then he added, "If it isn't too much to ask, it would help if these three guards could come with me."

The king laughed. He picked up a heavy, jeweled siver cup and tossed it to Paco. "Your wish is granted, wizard. Take this cup to remember how you have served your king."

Back in his own village, Paco's family was overjoyed at his return. The three guards served Paco and his family faithfully for many, many years. They told tales of Paco's magical deeds to anyone who would listen, even though none of the tales were true. The thieves cooked wonderful meals. They did all the wash. They cleaned the family's house, so no one in Paco's family ever had to work hard again. Paco's mother spent all of her days resting under a shady tree and praising her son. Everyone—even the former guards—was very happy.

So it came to pass that the clever Paco, who was never really a great wizard, kept his promise to return home with enough wealth to care for his whole family.